resurrection PERVERTS

HUNTER'S POINT

by Danny Hellman

RESURRECTION PERVERTS · HUNTERS POINT

STILL HERE.
THE LAST DEAD MAN ALIVE.

I'VE SETTLED INTO MYSELF
LIKE AN OLD STAR.
PROTECTED BY DISTANCE
FROM THE LIGHT OF OTHER STARS.

I PULL VOICES FROM THE DEEP.
FAINT RIPPLES ON THE SURFACE OF THE SEA
ECHOES OF THAT LAST DAY.

NHE
SOKE
HUZI
COMING UP IN OUR SECOND HOUR, FORMER FBI PROFILER EVE LAZAR GIVES US A PEEK INSIDE THE MIND OF THE Rx KILLER...
SOMETHING ELSE?

3W
REAKING:
GRAFTON SEX ROMP
...BUT FOR NOW, WE HAVE JUST A FEW MORE MINUTES WITH HARLOT MAGAZINE'S HARRY HOMBURG.
OH, I'M SORRY.
UM.
ANOTHER COKE, PLEASE.

LOOK, BONNIE--I'M USED TO BEING TREATED LIKE A LEPER BY HOLIER-THAN-THOU MEDIA TYPES LIKE YOU, BUT CAN WE PUT THINGS IN PERSPECTIVE?
BREAKING:
GRAFTON SEX
KISTANIS REFUSE TO G
WOULD YOU LIKE ME TO CHANGE THE CHANNEL?

I'M A BUSINESSMAN. I PROVIDE ENTERTAINMENT TO MY FELLOW MAN.
I'M NOT KILLING PEOPLE AND SHPRITZING THEM WITH SPRAY PAINT LIKE THIS Rx WACKO!
We
Ha
Pu
Ha

WHAT THAT GUY'S DOING IS REAL PERVERSION.
GRANTED, HE'S WHACKING SHOW BIZ HAS-BEENS AND B-LISTERS, NOT ACTUAL HUMANS, BUT STILL...
YEAH, I'VE GOT IT ON NOW, BUT THE DAMN MACHINE WON'T WORK WITH ME.
CAN YOU RECORD IT?
3W
HARRY HOMB
RIBAL WARLORDS PLE

I'M SURE THE VICTIMS' FAMILIES APPRECIATE YOUR WIT, BUT LET'S GET BACK TO YOUR DECISION TO PUBLISH THESE PHOTOS.
BACK IN THE 1980S, THE REAGAN WHITE HOUSE WORKED WITH CHRISTIAN FUNDAMENTALISTS TO PUT PEOPLE LIKE YOU BEHIND BARS.

NO JOKE. THEY SENT MY OLD MAN AWAY FOR A LITTLE WHILE.
I'LL BE DAMNED, THERE'S THE KID.
A LITTLE WHILE
SHOULD GRAFTON RES
NANOTECH: Can It Deliver?

BY PUBLISHING THESE PHOTOS NOW, AREN'T YOU HANDING THE WHITE HOUSE BACK TO THE REPUBLICANS WRAPPED IN A BIG, RED BOW?
IS HARRY HOMBURG AIDING AND ABETTING HIS NATURAL ENEMIES?
BONNIE, I HAVE NATURAL ENEMIES IN BOTH PARTIES.
You natu enemie
3

I'M A REGISTERED INDEPENDENT.
I'M NO FAN OF THE REPUBLICANS' MORAL HYPOCRISY, BUT I WON'T HAVE THE DEMOCRATS REDISTRIBUTING MY WEALTH, EITHER.
HARRY HOMBURG
3W
SALE!
PAULIE, CHANGE THE CHANNEL.
THERE'S KIDS IN THE STORE!

SHOULD GRAFTON RESIGN?
3W
FORGET THE POLITICS, THE GRAFTON SEX PICTURES ARE NEWS.
YOU'RE SEEING THE FIRST AMENDMENT IN ACTION, AND THAT'S WHAT MAKES PUBLISHING EXCITING FOR ME.
OLD MAN, I DON'T GIVE A FUCK WHO YOU'RE WITH!
JUST KEEP YOUR HANDS OFF MY SHIT!

I HAVEN'T SEEN THESE PICTURES, BUT IF YOUR PRESS RELEASE IS ACCURATE, I THINK IT'S SAFE TO SAY THAT THE PRESIDENT'S REELECTION BID IS DEAD IN THE WATER.
LOOK, BONNIE--- NO ONE KNOWS HOW THIS WILL PLAY OUT, BUT I'M HOPING OUR COUNTRY CAN FINALLY LET GO OF ALL ITS PURITANICAL BULLSHIT!
THESE PHOTOS SHOW ME THAT JIM GRAFTON'S NOT JUST SOME ANDROID WITH CAPPED TEETH AND AN EXPENSIVE HAIRCUT.
HE'S A VIRILE, WELL-ENDOWED HUMAN MALE, AND I THINK WE ALL WANT THAT IN OUR LEADERS, DON'T WE?

AND AGAIN, I'D LIKE TO APOLOGIZE TO OUR VIEWERS FOR MR. HOMBURG'S INAPPROPRIATE--
THIS SCANDAL PRESENTS AN OPPORTUNITY FOR US TO STEP OUTSIDE OUR ILLUSIONS AND SEE OURSELVES AS WE ARE.
SEX IS HARD-WIRED INTO OUR NATURE, SO WHAT'S THE BIG HANGUP ABOUT?
WHY DO WE WANT OUR LEADERS TO BE ROBOTIC DISNEYLAND SAINTS?
WHY CAN'T THE MADONNA ALSO BE A WHORE?

WE'RE NOT MACHINES. WE'RE ANIMALS WITH INSTINCTIVE DRIVES.
I'M WORKING HARD TO HELP THIS COUNTRY SHED ITS INVETERATE HYPOCRISY.
I'M DOING GOD'S WORK.
YOU PIECE OF SHIT!
I ORDERED YOU TO TURN THE TV OFF!
BELLMER
Carl Andre

BLOGGERS ARE SPECULATING ABOUT HOW YOU OBTAINED THESE PHOTOS.
IS AMERICA'S LAST PORN MOGUL TAKING CUES FROM THE VAST RIGHT WING CONSPIRACY?
THERE'S NO CONSPIRACY HERE.
I GOT A CALL FROM CELEBRITY PHOTOGRAPHER ARNIE KARAYAN, MY GOOD FRIEND FOR OVER THIRTY YEARS.
HE'D STRUCK GOLD, AND WE BOTH KNEW IT.

SMASH THE STATE!
THE ONLY THING I CONSPIRE TO DO IS TO MAKE MONEY, AND THAT'S WHAT I'LL BE DOING NEXT MONDAY WHEN THE NOVEMBER ISSUE OF HARLOT MAGAZINE HITS NEWSSTANDS.
3W
HARRY HOMBURG
SEE? WHAT DID I TELL YOU?
THIS IS EXACTLY HOW THEY OPERATE!
FUCKING LIZARD MEN.
PHILIP K. DICK
A MAZE OF DEATH

CAN YOU GIVE US---
SPEAKING OF MAKING MONEY, I KNOW MY HARLOT READERS WOULD LOVE TO SEE A CLASSY, ARTISTIC NUDE LAYOUT FEATURING BONNIE HERMANA.

WHILE I'M PRETENDING TO BE FLATTERED, CAN YOU TELL US HOW MR. KARAYAN MANAGED TO GET SO CLOSE TO JIM GRAFTON IN A MOMENT OF INTIMACY?
OKAY, I'LL TRY AGAIN TONIGHT, BUT DON'T HOLD YOUR BREATH.
HE'S ALREADY SAID "NO" TWICE.
GETTING CLOSE TO CELEBRITIES DURING THEIR UNGUARDED MOMENTS IS WHAT ARNIE DOES BEST.
THAT'S WHY HE GETS THE BIG BUCKS.
3W
SHOULD GRAFTON RESIGN?

BUT AREN'T PUBLIC FIGURES ENTITLED TO PRIVATE LIVES?
WE NEED TO BE RESPONSIBLE FOR OUR ACTIONS.
WE'RE IN AN AGE OF CELL PHONE CAMERAS AND SURVEILLANCE VIDEO.
WHEN YOU ENGAGE IN NUDE OUTDOOR FROLICS, GUESS WHAT, FOLKS?
SOMEBODY'S WATCHING!

DO WE EVEN WANT PRIVACY?
LOOK AT SOCIAL MEDIA, WHERE PEOPLE BROADCAST EVERY MORONIC THOUGHT.
THE ONLY PRIVATE PLACE LEFT IS THE SPACE BETWEEN OUR EARS, AND WITH MOST OF US, THAT'S JUST COBWEBS.
I'M SORRY, I DON'T KNOW WHERE I'M GOING WITH THIS.
CAM
CAM 8
VR4
VR5
VR6
SIGN?
TON RESIGN?
UCLA B BRUINS
GRAFTON'S TOAST.
WHY CAN'T SOMEONE SHOOT THIS CLOWN?

BEFORE WE LET YOU GO, PUBLICATIONS LIKE YOURS BLOSSOMED DURING THE SEXUAL REVOLUTION.
as the raphic gazine become levant?
TODAY, GIVEN OUR SEX-SATURATED CULTURE, AND AN AUDIENCE MOVING TOWARD DIGITAL MEDIA, HAS THE PORN MAGAZINE BECOME IRRELEVANT?
IS HARRY HOMBURG READY TO BE STUFFED AND DISPLAYED IN A MUSEUM?

RLOT
DEC 1970
MARTHA MITCHELL NUDE!
GIRLS OF THE WEATHER UNDERGROUND
CLEARLY THE INTERNET PRESENTS A CHALLENGE FOR TRADITIONAL PUBLISHERS, BUT THE HARLOT READER WON'T BE SEDUCED BY THIS DIGITAL MONSTER THAT'S DEVOURING MY AD REVENUE.
THE HARLOT READER IS A CONNOISSEUR WHO CHOOSES TIMELESS PLEASURES OVER FADS.
HARRY HOMBURG
YOU SCHOOL THAT BITCH, HARRY!
I NY
BUTT PARTY
HA

3W
ARE YOU TELLING
SHOULD GRAFTON RESIGN?
ARE YOU TELLING US THAT THE HARLOT READER ISN'T READY TO ENTER THE DIGITAL AGE?
THESE LINES ARE CRAZY. MY YOUNGEST SAYS I SHOULD DO ONLINE BANKING.
EVERYTHING HAPPENS INSIDE THESE COMPUTERS NOW.
SAMAEL

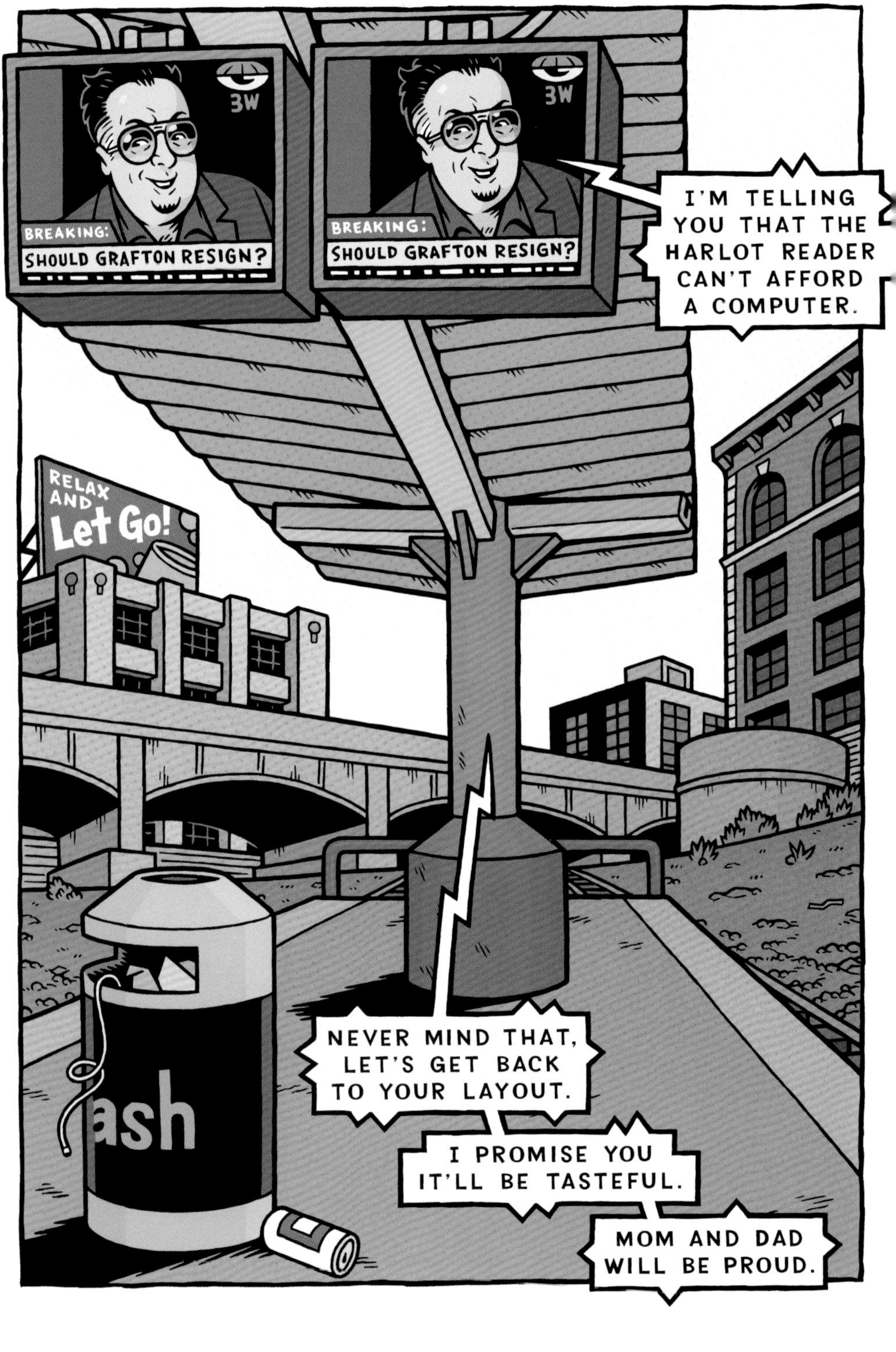
3W
BREAKING:
SHOULD GRAFTON RESIGN?
3W
BREAKING:
SHOULD GRAFTON RESIGN?
I'M TELLING YOU THAT THE HARLOT READER CAN'T AFFORD A COMPUTER.
RELAX AND Let Go!
ash
NEVER MIND THAT, LET'S GET BACK TO YOUR LAYOUT.
I PROMISE YOU IT'LL BE TASTEFUL.
MOM AND DAD WILL BE PROUD.

BIG PHARMA MIGHT ONE DAY INVENT A DRUG STRONG ENOUGH TO MAKE ME CONSIDER THAT OFFER.
UNTIL THEN, THANK YOU HARRY HOMBURG...
WE'LL TALK AFTER THE SHOW.

...PUBLISHER OF HARLOT MAGAZINE.
BELIEVE IT OR NOT, MY PRODUCER SWEARS HE'S NEVER MISSED AN ISSUE.
MAY HE LIVE FOREVER.

BREAKING:
GRAFTON SEX
CLIMATE SUMMIT FAILS TO RE
AND THERE I AM AGAIN!
GOD BLESS CABLE TELEVISION.

3W
RESIGN?
▲25.23 ▼76
I DON'T SEE MISS BRAND, BUT IF YOU'RE READY, THE OTHER TWO ARE HERE.
THAT'S GOOD.
I'D HATE TO SEE ASHLEY FACE BARB ALONE AND UNARMED.
PAPAGENO

SO, I GO TO PICK UP MY LUGGAGE, AND WHO DO I SEE ON THE TV TALKING TO BONNIE HERMANA?
I CAN'T STAND THAT WOMAN.
SO SANCTIMONIOUS.
PAPAGENO

I HAD TO RUN BACK TO THE GATE AND BEG THE STEWARDESS FOR A BARF BAG!
COME HERE, YOU DECREPIT MUMMY...

JIMMY, LISTEN. THIS GUY IS MACROBIONIC.
NO MENU...
...JUST BRING HIM A BOWL OF MOSS.

NAT, I DON'T KNOW IF THERE'S ANYTHING YOU CAN EAT ON THIS MENU!
SERIOUSLY, EVEN THE SALADS HAVE MEAT IN THEM.
BARBARA, MY SWEET.
WHAT, THEY CAN'T HOLD THE MEAT?

NAT, RELAX!
WE'LL JUST GET A PLATE SO YOU CAN POUR OUT ALL YOUR VITAMINS.
HARRY, YOU LOST YOUR BALL-BUSTING PRIVILEGES WHEN YOU HAD THAT BYPASS.
WHICH REMINDS ME, DID YOU QUIT SMOKING?

YOU BETTER BELIEVE I QUIT SMOKING.
AND IT WAS A STENT, NOT A BYPASS.
AT LEAST THEY LET ME DRINK WINE.
YOU LOOK TIRED.

I'M WIPED OUT.
THEY HAD ME IN THAT STUDIO AT 8AM.
AW, BABY NEEDS HIS NAPTIME?
ALL WORN OUT FROM YOUR EGO TRIP?

IT'S ALWAYS SO NICE WHEN YOU JOIN US FOR DINNER, BARB.

SHOULD GRAFTON RESIGN?
3W
YOU WERE HERE AT ABOUT THIS TIME LAST WEEK WEREN'T YOU?
UM, YEAH.
BLIND DATE.
SHE SWEARS SHE'LL MAKE IT THIS TIME.
KENNETH ANGER'S
HOLLYWOOD BABYLON

SHOULD
PAN ASIAN SUMM
WHY IS DATING SO STRESSFUL?
I DON'T KNOW.
SOMETIMES IT'S HARD TO WORK UP THE NERVE.

SO KID, BUSINESS AS GRIM AS I'VE HEARD?
WE'RE IN THE TOILET.
AD SALES ARE FLATLINING. ALL I'VE GOT COMING IN NOW IS LICENSING MONEY.
JUST BE GLAD YOU GOT OUT WHEN YOU DID.

WHAT HAVE I BEEN SAYING TO YOU FOR THIRTY YEARS?
KNOW YOUR READER.
WHO IS THE HARLOT READER?
HONESTLY, NAT...
...I THINK THE HARLOT READER GOT TAKEN OUT BY THE SAME METEOR THAT NAILED THE DINOSAURS.

EVERYTHING'S RIDING ON THESE GRAFTON PHOTOS.
IF WE DON'T SCORE BIG WITH THIS ISSUE, IT'S BLOODBATH TIME.
GOODBYE SANTA MONICA OFFICE.
HARRY, I REALLY WISH YOU'D TAKE ANOTHER LOOK AT THESE PRINTS TEESH SENT US.

YOU KNOW LEN HATES IT WHEN YOU DO THESE END-RUNS AROUND PHOTO.
AND I'VE SEEN THIS SET ALREADY.
THE GIRL IS TOO OLD!
WHAT DO YOU THINK, NAT?
LET'S SEE WHAT YOU'VE GOT HERE.

HAVE I TOLD YOU HOW TIRED I AM OF YOU AND TEESH CONNIVING TO TAKE MY MONEY?
THAT'S BULLSHIT, HARRY.

TEESH HAS A WALL FULL OF INTERNATIONAL AWARDS.
SHE'S HELPED US SELL A LOT OF MAGAZINES OVER THE YEARS.
BARB, I'M RUNNING A BUSINESS, NOT A WELFARE OFFICE FOR YOUR RETIRED STRIPPER'S CLUB!

FORGET THAT, WHAT'S HAPPENING WITH THOSE X-TERMINUS GUYS?
NOTHING'S HAPPENING.
I HAVEN'T HAD A CHANCE TO GO OVER THE CONTRACT WITH LEN.
THAT'S BECAUSE YOU AND THAT SUCCUBUS WITH A LIGHT METER ARE TOO BUSY DRAINING MY LAST VEIN!

BARB, REMIND ME.
WHY DO I KEEP YOU AROUND?
I DON'T KNOW.
GUILT OVER RUINING MY LIFE?

NAT, HAVE YOU EVER SEEN BARB'S LOFT?
DESIGNER FURNITURE. SPECTACULAR VIEWS. PRICELESS ART.
AND I KEEP SIGNING THE CHECKS.

SWEETIE, HERE'S WHAT I'D LIKE TO KNOW...
...WHEN YOU FINALLY SOBER UP AND REALIZE THAT ALL YOU'VE EVER DONE IS SHIT ON PEOPLE, ARE YOU GOING TO BE ABLE TO LIVE WITH YOURSELF?

WHAT DO YOU THINK OF THOSE PICTURES, NAT?
BARBARA, I'VE GOTTA AGREE WITH THE KID ON THIS ONE.
SHE'S PAST IT.

FUCKING PEDOPHILES.

SO IT'S LIKE WE'RE ALL CELLS INSIDE A GIANT BODY, RIGHT?
THAT'S SO FUNNY.
YOU SOUND JUST LIKE MY EX.
Rest Ro
HOLLYW
BABYLON
KENNE

RESIGN?
75 20
SO, IN THAT CONTEXT, WHAT IS FAME?
EGO GROWING OUT OF PROPORTION, DRAINING VITAL ENERGY FROM EVERYTHING THAT SURROUNDS IT?
CANCER.

EXACTLY.
THAT'S SO INTERESTING.
I REALLY MEAN IT!
HEY, HAVE YOU EVER READ THIS? IT REALLY HELPED ME PUT THINGS TOGETHER.
st Rooms
HUBBARD
DIANETICS

THERE SHE IS.
HELLO GORGEOUS!
HEY BIG GUY!

ASHLEY, I'D LIKE YOU TO MEET THE FORMER MRS. HOMBURG.
BARB BLOMEIER, HOW AWESOME IS THIS?
I USED TO WATCH YOU ON "EXTREME COUGAR CAGE: MIAMI" WHEN I WAS A WEE LASSIE!
THANK YOU, DEAR. YOU'RE TOO KIND.
UL THING TO LOVE WHAT DEATH CAN TO

AND THIS GENTLEMAN IS NAT SPECTER, WHO STARTED THE MAGAZINE WITH MY DAD IN THE LATE CRETACEOUS ERA.
HEYY-Y-Y!
KELP

NEXT MONTH, HE'S GONE TEN YEARS.
YOU KNOW THAT?
TEN YEARS.
S M T W T F S
YEAH, I KNOW.

NAT, HERE'S SOMETHING YOU'LL LIKE.
ASHLEY'S BEEN IN BAJA THE PAST MONTH SHOOTING "COLOSSUS: THE FORBIN PROJECT."
YOU DON'T SAY!
I INTERVIEWED THAT AUTHOR YEARS AGO.
ENGLISHMAN.
DONALD--- NO, DENNIS.
DENNIS JONES.
NAT'S THE WORLD'S OLDEST GEEK.

TIME TO SHOVE OVER AGAIN, BARB.
CHECK THIS OUT!
I DID THREE MONTHS WITH A THAI KICKBOXING TRAINER!

COLOSSUS WAS ORIGINALLY A COLD WAR STORY.
I IMAGINE THEY'VE CHANGED IT.
I'M PLAYING DR. CLEO MARKHAM WHO'S A TOTAL BADASS.
I HAVE TO DESTROY THIS CRAZY COMPUTER BEFORE IT ENSLAVES THE PLANET.
IT'S A FEARFUL THING TO LOVE WHAT DEATH
SHIT, I ALMOST FORGOT.
HEY, DAWN?
THOSE WHITE NOISE MACHINES SUCK.

SEND 'EM BACK.
YEAH, ALL THREE.
RIGHT, BYE.
HANSI GUDEGAST PLAYS MY BOYFRIEND, THE SCIENTIST WHO MADE COLOSSUS.
HE GETS INFECTED WITH A COMPUTER VIRUS AND TURNS EVIL.
THERE'S THIS HUGE BATTLE AT THE END WHERE I HAVE TO KILL HIM.
BRAD HAD US HANGING FROM WIRES IN FRONT OF A GREEN SCREEN FOR TWO WEEKS.
IT WAS NUTS!

THEY TOTALLY LEFT IT OPEN FOR A SEQUEL BECAUSE MY CHARACTER ALSO GETS INFECTED WITH THE VIRUS.
OH SHIT, SORRY.
SPOILER ALERT!
HEY, THERE'S ALWAYS MORE MONEY TO BE MADE.
WHO'S YOUR DIRECTOR?
IT'S A FEARFUL THING TO LOVE WHAT DEATH CAN TOUCH
KELP
S M T W T F S

BRAD TORVALD.
HE DID "BURNING THE MOON" AND "HIGH PRIESTESS."
HARRY INTRODUCED US AT CANNES LAST YEAR!
THE FIRST HALF OF "BURNING THE MOON" WAS GOOD, BUT THEN IT GOT SO SILLY.
PEOPLE DON'T WANT INTELLIGENT SCIENCE FICTION ANYMORE.

HONEY, I HAVE NO DOUBT YOU WERE PICKED FOR YOUR ACTING ABILITIES, BUT THAT DOUCHEBAG TORVALD HAS BEEN SLOWLY TUNNELING HIS WAY UP HARRY'S ASS FOR YEARS NOW.
BEHAVE YOURSELF, BARBARA.

NO, SHE'S RIGHT!
BRAD'S TOTALLY YOUR STALKER.
HE NEVER SHUTS UP ABOUT THAT FILM PROJECT HE WANTS TO DO ABOUT YOU.
WELL, HE'S NOT GETTING SIGN OFF FROM ME UNTIL HE FIXES HIS SCRIPT.
I KNOW I'M AN ASSHOLE, BUT I'M NOT THE FUCKING MARQUIS DE SADE!
OH, I DON'T KNOW.
KELP

ANYWAY, I'VE GOTTA GO PONDER THE VOID.
WHEN THE GIRL COMES BACK TELL HER TO BRING ME A NEW YORK STEAK MEDIUM RARE.

I'VE SOLD A FEW SCRIPTS TO HOLLYWOOD.
LET ME TELL YOU, FOR REAL TORTURE, THERE'S NO HELL LIKE DEVELOPMENT HELL.
I COUNT SIX BRAIN CELLS IN THIS ONE.
FOR ONE OF YOUR PLAYTHINGS, THAT'S THREE ABOVE AVERAGE.
BIG GUY.
I SAID BEHAVE.

HEY, YOU DON'T THINK YOU'RE GETTING STOOD UP AGAIN?
OR MAYBE YOU JUST CAME TO SEE ME?

Rest Room
L. RON HUBBARD
DIANETICS
DIANETICS
THIS IS ABOUT SPACE ALIENS CONTROLLING OUR MINDS, RIGHT?
I'M SORRY, THAT'S JUST TOO CRAZY.
EXCUSE ME.

HARRY

SORRY, KID.
PARDON THE SMOKE.
NO SMOKING

I BEAR WITNESS TO THE P-PESTILENCE UPON THE EARTH.
ONE-WORLD
EXCUSE ME?

I AM HIS SCALPEL, WHICH CUTS AWAY CORRUPT TISSUE.
NO SMOKING
WHOA, HEY-Y-Y...

I AM THE...
I AM...

SPRAY PAINT FUMES
AND EASY LISTENING
MUSIC.

NO SMOKING
THE PAIN SUBSIDES.
Rx
A SOUND LIKE RUSHING AIR DROWNS OUT THE MUZAK AND THE PUKING NOISES.

A HEAP OF BLOODY RAGS LIES NEXT TO THE TOILET.
IT HURTS TO LOOK AT IT.

THE FUMES CARRY ME UP.
FAN BLADES PULL ME THROUGH THE CEILING VENT.

TEMPUS
PAPA

END
NO STANDING ANYTIME

Time To Come Home!
NU•LIFE REALTY

3

AQUAVIT
STEP UP TO THE NEXT LEVEL
DAILY NEWS
EXCLUSIVE:
MARK OF A KILLER

MITED
TIME
WHO'S THERE?

WHEN YOU FLY WITH US YOU'RE WITH FAMILY
3W
HARRY HOMBURG
DAD!
JESUS, YOU LOOK GREAT!
IT'S NICE TO SEE YOU, HAROLD.

Point Avenue
HARRY HO
WHERE ARE WE?
THERE ARE SIGNS EVERYWHERE.
JUST TAKE A LOOK AROUND.
WHAT WILL YOU LEAVE TO THEM?

THIS IS SOME FUCKED-UP DREAM.
DAILY NEWS
MARK OF A KILLER
COME THIS WAY.
IT'S ALMOST HERE.

enue
NO, JUST HOLD ON A MINUTE.
SOMETIMES MORE ISN'T BETTER
THERE'S NOTHING TO BE AFRAID OF, HAROLD.
FOLLOW ME.

DAD, WAIT.
THERE'S SOMETHING I WISHED I COULD TELL YOU FOR A LONG TIME.

I'M SORRY ABOUT WHAT HAPPENED.
WITH THE BUSINESS, I MEAN.
I'M SORRY YOU HAD TO GO.
The Brands You Love!

I MADE MY CHOICE.
AND IT DOESN'T MATTER NOW.

THE ONLY---
GOD DAMN IT.
WHAT IS IT?
WHAT'S WRONG?

SOME...
...SOME
SHITBAGS.
THEY
WANT TO
SEE YOU.

Enue
SHITBAGS?
WHAT SHITBAGS?
I DON'T KNOW, HAROLD...
...BUT YOU'RE GONNA HAVE TO WAIT HERE.

TAKE CARE OF YOURSELF.
WHERE ARE YOU GOING, DAD?

DAD!!

RESURRECTION PERVERTS · HUNTERS POINT

to be continued...
©2017 Danny Hellman